PEEK-A-BOO PENGUIN
Colours
and
Shapes

Ruth Owen

Consultant: Jillian H

D0258624

QED Publishing

Peek-a-boo Penguin is picking flowers in his garden. He is picking **red** flowers.

Can you point to all the **red** flowers for Peek-a-boo?

Do you see something
else that is **red**?

3

Lots of birds visit
Peek-a-boo's garden.
Peek-a-boo likes the
blue birds best.

Point to all the **blue** birds
in Peek-a-boo's garden.

Do you see a **red** bird?

4

Some colourful bugs live in Peek-a-boo's garden.

 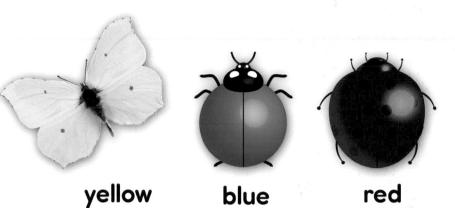

yellow   **blue**   **red**

Which ladybird isn't **red**? Can you say what **colour** it is?

Can you find two bugs in this row that look exactly the same? What colour are they?

It is autumn in
Peek-a-boo's garden.

He is wearing a **green** scarf.

Peek-a-boo is collecting
some **brown** leaves.

Match Peek-a-boo's
leaves to the same leaves
in the big picture.

What things can you point
to that are **brown**?

Look around your room. Can you spot something **green** or **brown**?

What **green** things can you spot?

7

Peek-a-boo likes to work in his garden.
He is wearing his **orange** hat.

He is wearing his **pink** apron.

Look at Peek-a-boo's garden tools.
What **colour** is the watering can?
Point to the **orange** tools.

Peek-a-boo's favourite garden friends
are the **grey** squirrels.

Let's count all the **grey** squirrels
in Peek-a-boo's garden!

9

It is night-time in Peek-a-boo's garden.
Everything looks **black**.

Try to spot these things in
Peek-a-boo's night-time garden.

It is snowing in Peek-a-boo's garden.

Peek-a-boo has made
a **white** snowman.

Look at the **white** snowflakes.
Can you find pairs of snowflakes that match?

Look at all the different shapes on Peek-a-boo's patio. Peek-a-boo is standing on a **square** shape.

Show Peek-a-boo how to get to his deckchair by stepping only on **squares**.

12

Peek-a-boo wants to feed his fish.  He is holding a box of fish food in the shape of a **rectangle**.

The fish live in a pond that is the shape of a **rectangle**. Which path takes Peek-a-boo to the correct pond?

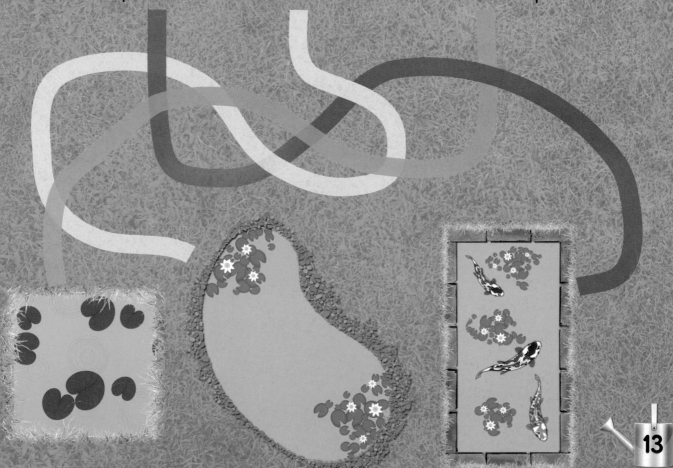

Peek-a-boo is playing with hoops.
The hoops are **circles**.

Look at Peek-a-boo's other toys.
Are there any more **circles**?

14

Peek-a-boo is having a picnic.
He is eating a sandwich.
The sandwich is the shape of a **triangle**.

Can you
see some
other **triangles**?

Peek-a-boo is building a garden shed!
He has lots of pieces of wood
in different shapes.

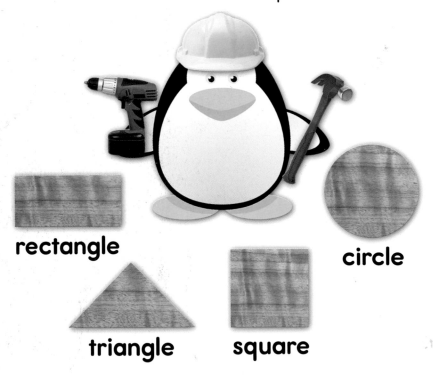

rectangle

triangle

square

circle

Look at Peek-a-boo's shed.
Do you see a big **square**?
Can you find a small and a big **triangle**?
Point to a **rectangle**.

Look around the room you are in. Can you spot a **square**?

What shape is the window?

17

Peek-a-boo has painted his new shed.
Can you match each paint pot
to the same colour on the shed?
Say the colours as you find them.

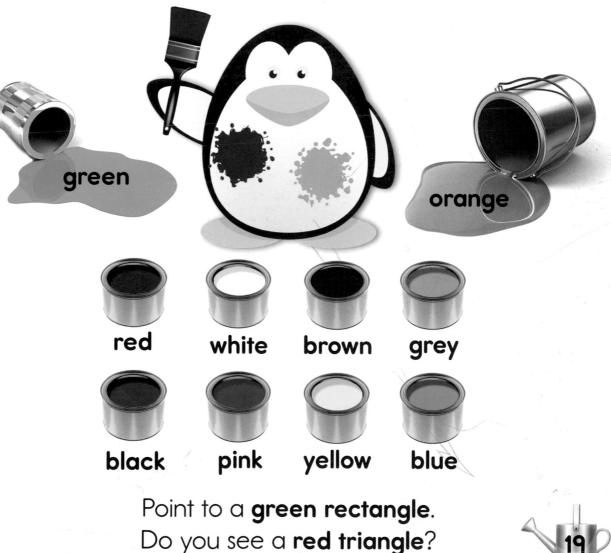

green

orange

red   white   brown   grey

black   pink   yellow   blue

Point to a **green rectangle**.
Do you see a **red triangle**?

19

lettuces

This is Peek-a-boo's vegetable garden.

potatoes

Look at the **green** lettuces.
What shape is the lettuce bed?

cabbages

Can you find
a **circle**?

carrots

Do you see some **yellow** vegetables?

corn

pumpkins

What colour are the vegetables that are growing in a **square**?

More fun with Peek-a-boo!

Now look back through your book. Let's help Peek-a-boo find some more colours and shapes.

Peek-a-boo wants to pick **red** and **yellow** flowers. Can you find Peek-a-boo some **yellow** flowers in your book?

Look for a **green** animal that lives in Peek-a-boo's garden.

Do you see something **blue** in your room?

22

Look out of the window. Can you see a **rectangle**?

Look through your book and spot as many **squares** as possible!

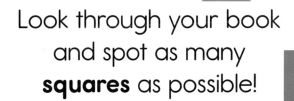

Peek-a-boo is hungry. Find him something to eat in your book that is the shape of a **circle**.

Look for a **yellow square** in Peek-a-boo's garden.

Can you find a **pink triangle** on his shed?

23

Notes for parents and teachers

The activities in this book are designed to introduce children to the important concepts of colours and shapes. The emphasis is on making learning fun, by using an engaging character to capture and focus the interest of young children. The book will help children to recognize a range of colours and to distinguish between common shapes.

Sit with the child and read each page to them. Allow time for the child to think about the activity. Encourage them to talk about what they are doing as they carry out the activity. Praise all attempts. If the child is hesitant, show the child how to begin by demonstrating the first part of the activity yourself.

Remember to keep activities short and to make them fun. Stop while your child is still interested. Avoid times when your child is tired or distracted, and try again another day. Children learn best when they are relaxed and enjoying themselves. It's best to help them to experience new concepts in small steps, rather than to do too much at once.

Use this book as a starting point for activities that your child could carry out at home or when out and about. Some ideas that you could try are:

- Play "Where's Peek-a-boo?" after each activity.

- Encourage your child to choose clothes to wear that match the colour of an item you have chosen.

- Invite your child to help you sort washing into dark and light items.

- Go on a shapes walk, and ask your child to look for things that are shaped like a square or circle.

- Cut out different coloured card into a variety of shapes and ask your child to sort the card into different shapes, or to find shapes of a particular colour.

Created by: Ruby Tuesday Books
Designer: Emma Randall

Copyright © QED Publishing 2011

First published in the UK in 2011 by
QED Publishing
A Quarto Group company
226 City Road
London EC1V 2TT

www.qed-publishing.co.uk

A catalogue record for this book is available from the British Library.

ISBN 978 1 84835 598 9

Printed in China